Advance Praise for
Las Criaturas

"There is an awareness that, nestled within our dormant DNA, we have our own monster within, just waiting for the chance to be free. Leticia Urieta's *Las Criaturas* is the culmination of all those stories. We are lucky to have this book."

— **jo reyes-boitel**,
author of *mouth* and *Michael + Josephine*

"*Las Criaturas* is a visceral incantation of memory and ancestral knowledge that blends horror and awe, myth and fairytale. In this stunning collection, Leticia Urieta explores the monstrous and the divine to re-embody the power of womanhood into its ever-present, beautiful, hybrid forms."

— **Natalia Sylvester**,
author of *Chasing the Sun* and *Everyone Knows You Go Home*

"In *Las Criaturas*, Leticia Urieta hones the conventions of folklore and mythology to center girls & women in a present context. Otherworldly and musical, *Las Criaturas* positions the monstrous as a form of power and place of refuge, firmly asking readers the pertinent questions: "Who creates the monsters? How do las criaturas that pervade our past, present, and future find justice?" Urieta has gifted us a daring and playful new work that points us in the right direction."

— **Reyes Ramirez**,
author of *The Book of Wanderers*

LAS CRIATURAS

FLOWERSONG
PRESS

by Leticia Urieta

FlowerSong Press
Copyright © 2021 by Leticia Urieta
ISBN: 978-1-953447-83-8
Library of Congress Control Number: 2021947666

Published by FlowerSong Press
in the United States of America.
www.flowersongpress.com

Cover Art by Elaine Almeida
Cover Design by Priscilla Celina Suarez
Author Photo Credit: Ramiro Urieta
Set in Adobe Garamond Pro

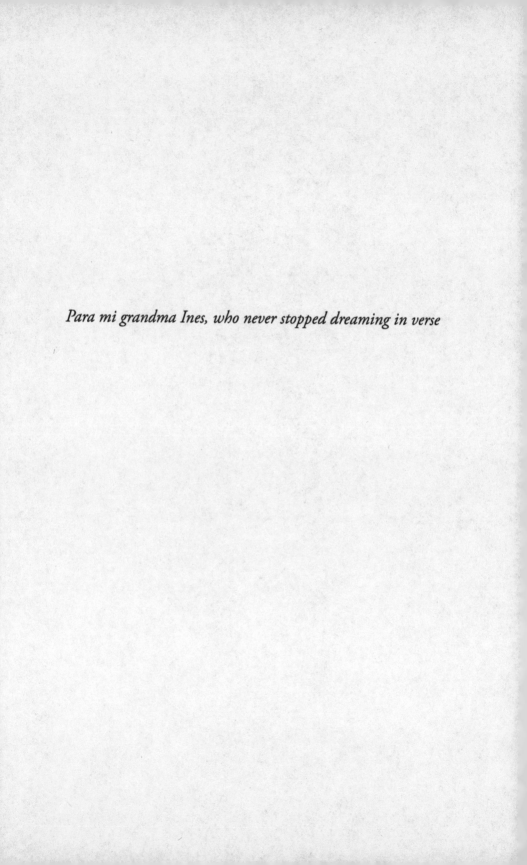

Para mi grandma Ines, who never stopped dreaming in verse

"Kiss me, sister, as we did in the old times. When we were a coven of sisters, coiled together like adders, like adders in the sands of Egypt, like hawks over Golgotha, like all things that come together and find strength as one."

— **Evelyn Poole**, *Penny Dreadful*

"And this criatura is always a creator-hag, or a Death goddess, or a maiden in descent-she is both friend and mother to all those who have lost their way, all those who need a learning, all those who have a riddle to solve, all those out in the forest or the desert wandering and searching."

— **Clarissa Pinkola Estes**,
Women Who Run with the Wolves:
Myths and Stories of the Wild Women Archetype

Contents

Part 1

Part 2

Part 3

Contents

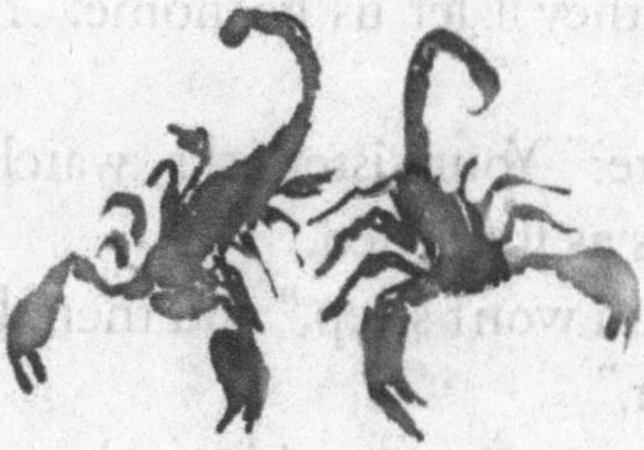

Part 1

THE MONSTER

"The gates are there to protect us," you tell her. You both peer through the wire mesh to the woods beyond the compound.

"When it's time, they'll let us go home." Not home across the border, you hope.

"What's back there?" Your sister asks, watching a flock of crows swarm out of the trees as if startled.

"I can't tell you, you won't sleep," and then, leaning down in your sister's ear, "A monster."

"¿De veras?" Those eyes go as wide as the gaps in the fence, you could poke a finger through the brown irises.

"A monster, that's what they say."

That's how you get your sister to stop crying, to accept the cramped portables with five other mothers and their children where you sleep, because you can't leave.

"What kind of monster is it?" she asks.

"They won't say what it looks like, but I imagine it has thick claws with sharp ends that slash, fur all over its body, like the kind a wild pig has, very bristly. It has a long snout, with fangs for cutting and crunching, and I bet it is as tall as the trees. Watch how they move." Your sister watches the trees sway. "It blends into the woods, and when people try to run away, they get lost. Then, it's too late." There is a pleasure in the telling, in seeing your sister's fists clench in fear around the chain of the swing set. Soon though, you release the tension in her with a rub across her little back, sturdy and warm, the kind that has survived leaving everything behind, and now this.

"Don't worry, Princesa. Soon the man will come with the papers that have the spell for our release. After that, we won't need to hide from the monster anymore." You can't tell if she believes any of this, if her believing makes this all worse. She is seven, too old to believe in these stories, but her body relaxes in the swing at the telling of it, and lets herself be pushed back and forth until it's time to go back to the cafeteria for the evening meal.

Outside those gates, your life continues without you.

You've been there for six months.

You have a toothache but won't tell your mother. The doctors here might make it worse either way. Sometimes they give other kids antibiotics and medicines that make them sick. "It's not an emergency," you tell yourself. You brush around it and feel the nerve pulsing. Your mother would not hesitate to take you to the dentist if you were on the outside. But you're not, so you let the tooth hurt, this rebellious piece of yourself which is unwilling to fall in line.

The waiting eats Mamí up until her bones appear under the outline of her shirts. She gets stomach aches from food; every vegetable from a can, overcooked and under seasoned, and meat that is mostly gristle and fat. Soon, she stops forcing it down. "I am doing it for a reason. If I don't eat, people will see how wrong it is to lock us up," she tells you. Confusion sets in. How will not eating make anyone see her if she wastes away to nothing?

The waiting keeps you both up at night.

"What if we have to go back?" you ask the darkness, ears pressing against it to hear your mother's response. Sometimes Mamí has no answer. A shadow takes form, stalks across the window as you try to fall to sleep. It scrapes against the glass like it wants inside, and you can see the claws extending toward you. The shadow grows long in the light of the moon, reaches for you, selecting you out of all of them and slips into your throat. The fear of going back eats you up, its claws digging into your stomach, reaching up into your chest and tearing at your lungs. You know that Mamí feels the same. You are comforted by the skin on her arm which is still soft, but going loose against you.

You used to see in the newspaper the signs with 'Ilegals Go Home!' written on them and other messages like "English Only" and "Secure Our Borders!" that seemed to say that if all of you were gone, the country could return to its former greatness.

Here, there isn't much to read. You used to be able to bring books home by the armload from the school library. The librarian was an understanding woman, and she spoke Spanish. She showed you the books in Spanish, and when you read almost all of those, the librarian encouraged you to read the new books in English that she ordered. Some books she gave you even had English and Spanish together, switching back and forth on each page like feet hopscotching from side to side, guided by the same brain. In eighth grade, you still loved the bilingual readers, but when you could read in English, a whole new world of stories opened up for you.

In here, your brain stagnates like water in a dirty puddle, filming over with dirt and flies. You have to make your own stories, on the playground where Mamí cannot hear.

"Where did the monster come from?" Your sister is at the top of the slide, calling down to you.

"It's always been here."

She slides down with a whoosh, feet crunching on gravel and then running back around to get another turn before someone els comes.

"We were safe before in our apartment. Why did they bring us here where the monster is?"

You watch your sister's brown curls sweep back behind her as she goes down, her voice breathless this time. She runs back again.

"When you come from somewhere else, they have to make sure you're good enough to be here. If we listen, and follow the rules, then the man comes with the spell, and if the spell works, then we can leave without being fed to the monster."

Can they do that?"

You yank her feet down and you both fall to the ground, hugging her to you.

"That's not going to happen to us."

But that night, you dream of you both at the top of the slide, unable to stop yourselves from falling into the sharp toothed gaping mouth at the bottom, black eyes gleaming back at your own.

In school, the classes are divided amongst a few different teachers. You're in the upper grades class, but there are still kids of all different ages there. The class takes place part of the day in Spanish, part in English, a weird hodgepodge of reading workbooks, copying sentences and language activities. Because you know English better than most, your teacher gives you a packet of math problems to do. They're for sixth graders, equations you've mastered two years ago, but you do them anyway, and then read the battered copy of "A to Z Mysteries" that you liked back when you were first learning the language.

Your teacher, white woman, is sweaty, always up and moving, trying to assist each student in a new state of panic or boredom. You can't blame a teacher for not teaching when she's busy just trying to keep things from falling apart. The girl who sits next to you, a recent arrival from Honduras, finishes her work quickly and says "I hear your English," and moves closer to you, wanting you to read the mystery book aloud, leaning her head on her hands in an expectant pose. You do, and can almost see your own words seeping into her ears and floating up into her brain.

Sometimes you sit together on the floor by the window on the cold tile so that your friend can follow along with the words. Even if they have no meaning yet, this girl sweeps her finger under each line and mumbles along. In the noisy chaos of the classroom, the only place besides the playground where kids are allowed to be loud, you go undisturbed for at least an hour. She tells you stories from Honduras, of their family and who were left behind.

"We take a train to get here," she says and mimics the snaking movement of the train with her hand.

"Why do they call it that?"

"It is so long. Come all the way from Honduras to Mexico. People die."

You ask her to explain, but she doesn't have the words in English, and you have have trouble remembering the words in Spanish to describe why people die on the way to los estados unidos. You've been speaking English too long. Instead, you begin to teach her words in English you think she may need to know: more, help, please, cold, sick, hurts.

In return for her story, you tell her about the apartment that Tia is keeping clean for your return.

In this home, your American home, Mamí prepared the meals,

even after working all day. The beans would bubble on the stove, and the apartment smelled like azafran, ajo and cebolla, and the seasoned rice filled your hungry bellies after a long day at school and the bus ride home. You could smell it even after the dishes were soaking in the sink and then the three of you would crowd together on the rented couch to watch TV. Your Mamí liked watching those silly game shows on Telemundo, but switched away when the news came on. Seeing bodies lying in the street and hanging from bridges gave your sister nightmares.

In the old house in Michoacan, the three of you left behind your tios, your primos and your abuela. You remember when it wasn't safe to walk home alone anymore or at night. Sometimes there were bodies left on the side of highways, and it seemed that your family always knew someone who had lost someone to the narcos. The older familia always said, "si no te metes, nada te pasará," but it always seemed like there was more to that story. A boy that you knew from the neighborhood started working for them. He was only twelve. You watched him walk around with wads of cash tucked inside his jeans, refusing to talk to anyone from the old vecindad, and somehow that hurt more than his arrogant swagger and how he threatened the little kids who walked by him. When you saw him in town, he would look past you, as though you hadn't shared books at school the year before.

That was when Mamí decided to move you all away, all the way north across the frontera. Mamí's sister got her a job at a Mexican restaurant making tortillas. After a day's work, they both came home smelling like maiz y harina, laughing when they walked through the door, even though their feet ached from standing all day, as if those moments made up for the years separated by fence and miles.

But Tia has papers. On the way to school, Mamí was driving too fast, late to drop you off, running late for work, when a policeman pulled her over. Her hands shook on the steering wheel, knowing she had no license to give the officer. He leaned through the window, staring her down, and, looking at you in the front seat, your sister in the back, both strapped in, hands on your laps, quiet, and still he had you get out and sit in the backseat of his car while he drove you to the police station. You sat with her sister on a wooden bench outside the room where they took Mamí to talk to another officer whose jacket said ICE. It was freezing, sitting on the bench, and you thought that maybe the ICE man made it cold to punish people, though you couldn't think what Mamí had done wrong. You remember now that your greatest sadness was missing the fifteen minutes in the morning that your teacher liked to spend reading aloud. That week the class was reading *Esperanza Rising*. As you sat on the bench, holding your little sister's clammy hand, you pictured the cover of the book, of Esperanza flying above the fields, away from the pain of not belonging and into the cloudless sky.

Tears hang off your eyelashes. Your nueva amiga wipes them away with her thumb.

The monster stays quiet for a time.

Since Mamí doesn't come to meals anymore, you eat with your friend and her little brother and mother, sitting together on the benches that run along the tables like it could be home. Her mother spoons applesauce into her baby's mouth and you laugh when he smiles and it sloops out the sides of his mouth. You pinch your sister's cheeks and remind her of when she was like that, too little to do anything but stare and smile. Even the woman guard with the long black hair tied back so tight it must hurt smiles at you from the corner of the room by the door. You wonder if she has a baby at home, if under her uniform her belly is still soft from carrying him around. You smile back, wanting her to see that you are good, you are normal, like the rest of families here.

Back in the dormitory, your sister sits on the lower bunk and lets you brush away the tangles in her hair.

"You like them more than me," she says.

She turns to look at you behind her, and you force her head forward to work through a knot at the base of her skull.

"They've been nice to us. Sometimes I need someone to talk to my own age. Just like Mamí has Tia to talk to."

"I don't care. Mamí is lonely too. Just like me."

"Mami is causing trouble," you hiss. You wrench the brush down until her head falls backwards.

"Don't brush so hard!"

How easy it would be, you think, to crunch through her small neck like a wolf does, so she could leave this place once and for all. This idea makes you jump away from her, afraid of your hands so close to her fragile body.

"Go outside for a while preciosa.."

She ties up her hair, now free of tangles, and runs off where the others are playing. You lay back on the bed and clutch the hairbrush to your chest. You are shaking.

Las guardias stand watch, in the yard, outside the dormitories, in the cafeteria, standing guard for some latent violence you were so sure they would never see. Now, your story makes a fool of you.

Mamí calls the lawyer that Tia found for us. Papers were filed, but no court date has been set. You ask your mother to explain what this means about returning home.

"Not yet," she tells you. The guard reminds her that other people are waiting for their phone calls. Mamí returns to the dormitories and asks not to be followed. She always shared her news before, but now there is a space between you both while you continue to wait.

That night, you push away from her clasping hands until she clenches them around your wrists and wrenches you around to face her.

You feel full of the roiling, hairy hatred that time here is creating. A look passes between you both in the dark.

"What is wrong with you?!" she whispers.

There is something gleaming in her eyes even where the round cheeks have shrunk and the sockets are shadowed. This is Mamí's plan, to be consumed, no matter what happens to her daughters. You push her back to the edge of the bed you share and flip towards the window. There are no shadows on the moon. They are living inside.

Your friend from class is leaving with her mother and baby brother. She gives you a hug while her mother packs one small duffel bag with the few things they brought with them, and tells you she will write to you, and that maybe they will visit once you are released. Their family is the first to leave so quickly. Others have left, but not because they are allowed to stay in the country. Some are sent back from where they came on one big bus. You wish you could believe that you will see her again.

After saying goodbye, you don't feel the same. The sympathetic guard who smiled at you leads you back to the classroom where you lay your head on your desk and fall asleep, unnoticed by the teacher. The creature inside reaches out a hairy arm through your open mouth. It slashes the teacher across the face, it busts open the classroom door and chews through the neck of the guards standing watch at the entrance, using your own teeth to crunch through their necks and feel the hot spray of blood in your mouth. Your monster feet lead you into the cool overhang of trees. For all you know, that is where you belong.

Your face aches against the cold wooden desk when you awake and see drool mixed with blood has seeped onto your arm and smeared across the sleek wood. No one has noticed that you were asleep. You open your workbook to a random page and run your finger beneath the words, wishing there was still someone to read them to.

At recess, kids of all ages meander around the gravel playground. For once, you think that you would rather be inside than have to look out and see your freedom so close. The younger class if already outside and you search out your sister, who is fighting with another girl for a turn on the swing. She leans close to the girl, hands clenched like claws around the chain of the swing, and whispers something to her. That girl runs off crying to another corner of the yard. Your sister settles herself comfortably onto the seat and pushes off, content with what she's done. You walk over and begin to push her. She watches the trees.

"It's close now," she says.

"What?"

"The monster."

You keep pushing, listening to your sister over the cries of the other kids.

"I feel it."

"What did you say to that girl?"

Your sister continues to pump her legs back and forth while you push her just a little higher.

"She wouldn't stop, so I told her that the monster was going to get her if she was gonna be so mean."

You jerk the swing to a stop and kneel in front of her.

"That was our secret. You can't tell people that."

"But I hate waiting for the man to come to set us free."

"I know, but we have to wait. There's nothing else we can do."

"I don't want to be the princess if I have to wait here for someone else to come and save me. I wish I were a monster too, with a long tail and spikes and teeth that chomp so I could kill that monster. Then we could go home." She gnashes her teeth like she is chewing bones between them and raises her arms above her head to show her ferocity. For a moment, your sister's eyes turn an inky black and you think of the book you've read "Donde viven los monstruos," about the boy who acted like a monster to his parents and became the king of the monsters himself. Still, in the end he went back when he became tired of that game.

You snatch her arms into a painful grip and pull them down so that you are face to face.

"No eres monstruo, ni princesa. You are just you," you growl while your sister cries.

Mami is upset with you later. As weak as she is, getting out of bed makes her nauseous, so she stays most of the day in the nursing area lying on the blue padded cots with a blanket over her. The mother guard who smiles at you escorts both you and your snotty, crying sister inside. Her cries ring off the sterile, freezing white walls. Mami rolls on her side to face you and strokes your sister's hair to calm her.

"What did you say?" Her interrogative tone is for you.

"She was acting bad," you say. Your sister continues to cry and shake her head in denial; her tears cascade all over her shirt. Mami looks back at you.

"Look what you did. You should be taking care of her." Even in anger her voice lacks exclamation. Mami closes her eyes and puts her hand over her face to block out the room. She gives up on the conversation.

"Come out girls, let's let your Mom rest," the mother guard says. She puts her hand around your shoulder and you don't resist. Your sister breathes hard from her crying, but she lets you wipe the underside of her nose with your shirt sleeve. Instead of taking you back to the playground, the guard leads you down the winding hallway to the entrance to the kitchens where you aren't allowed to go. She knocks and the cafeteria cook emerges.

"These two need ice cream." The cook nods, lets the door swing shut, then returns with two ice cream sandwiches. The mother guard thanks her and gives you both one. They are straight out of the freezer and still hard, just like you like them. You help your sister peel back the wrapping paper and take a bite. It freezes your teeth in the most satisfying way.

"Maybe we should start feeding your Mom these since you like them so much. The nurse says she's going to have to start eating again either way," the mother guard tells you. She doesn't know Mami, her insistence to see something through. You love and hate this quality in her. By the time you reach to the door that opens onto the playground, the guard has made sure you both have finished your ice cream and takes your wrappers so that none of the other kids see the evidence of her kindness and complain.

"Thank you Señora," you say, and nudge your sister to say the same as she licks the melted ice cream from her hands. This is the first time you have thanked someone in this place and meant it.

In the evening after dinner, alone in the dormitory while the other families play around in the recreation room, you sit and hold a doll your friend gave you before she left. It reminds you of the dolls you could buy at the market back home, the bright colored dresses and woven black braids on top of her head. The night is clear, and you hold the doll up to the moonlight to see her smiling, vacant face. You wonder if your friend kept a similar doll for herself, and that when she looks into its eyes, she can see you looking back. In the dark you whisper to the doll like speaking messages through a walkie-talkie, hoping someone is listening on the other side.

Outside the window, beyond the fence, the trees sway in the wind. You think that you see a shadow slinking back behind the canopy, a defeated monstrous form that goes away to wait.

OFFERING TO THE SKY

In the morning we tied you, our baby, to balloons and watched you float up and away from us into the gray sky, floating straight to heaven.

We packed you in hampers, in baskets, tied balloons to chairs for the older ones and strapped you in with severed car seat belts and twine, letting our collective hope lift you away from this place.

Attached to your clothes were notes in as many languages as we could think of pleading for safe passage for our little ones. We even made sure to give you white balloons. White for clouds. White for peace. White for disappear.

In the dark before dawn we kissed our sleeping crying babies. We brought you to the roof to cast you all away. All around us, other mothers and fathers, grandmothers and uncles wiped their eyes clean and tied the balloon strings tight. Who knew who sent their little one up first? No one wanted to be the first or the last.

Some balloons weren't fastened right; the children never made it off the ground, got stuck in trees, and we were all afraid to hear the morning ripped open by your screams. Finally, we saw our neighbor's children ride the wind into the clouds and knew it would work. There, on our cracked roof, we pressed our lips to your fuzzy forehead. You were warm, tucked so carefully into your basket with blankets all around you. You didn't know yet what goodbye meant. We never taught you that.

Your father lifted the basket onto his shoulders while I arranged the balloon strings. With one great heave you, our son, were up and away. You would not hear our voices again, or recognize our faces on the news.

MEDUSA BUYS EYELINER

Medusa picks out eyeliner at the pharmacy
she buys press on nails that sparkle.
She hasn't worn brightness on her body since
she painted her mouth red. Her father smeared it
across her face, paint that attracts unruly gods.
Her Tinder profile reads-*I am a betrayed woman*,
not looking for fake friends, the kind that say
they are saving you as they cut you down.
Medusa won't wear white any longer, her dress is stained
from kneeling at the temple of strong women.
Her date says he will meet her at a bar. She sits
on the edge of her bed, swipes through profiles
on her phone. The voices of her sisters echo--
Let them come to you.
Before her date, the hair stylist tries
to flat iron her hissing curls. They snap and bite,
rearrange themselves in strike mode. She pays
for this, wishing she trusted the best way to care for herself.
Her cave has a reflecting pool, her mirror.
It is myth that she cannot see herself. Her shaky hand
runs the charcoal pencil around her lids, she embraces the darkness.
After their date, she lets him lie in her bed, staring up
at the stalactites pointing down daggers. His hand rests
on her soft belly, he begs her to look him in the eye.
She lines his stone body with the others, a circle
around the pool. The next message she gets is a
tenderness. A girl asks for a picture. Medusa takes a selfie,
let's camera become a mirror that won't
break under her stare.

La Mujer Alacrán

Un pico no mas, and his venom was inside her. In the night, when the bed was an oven, he rolled on top of her, she felt the sting against her back, pain spreading towards her thighs, and still amidst her cries he felt the need to finish.

Amidst the kisses and frantic hands, he wouldn't stop, and she felt the pain, the invasion just as she did the sting of the scorpion, one of many that folded themselves between her sheets, inside her shoes, in the corners and cracks. When it rained in the summer, they all came inside to look for sanctuary. Some were still clear brown, others black as the desert shadows. She thought she had grown cautious enough, known when to shake out her sheets and protect her body from the sting. She thought they could cohabitate.

After this boy left her shivering, she went to clean herself. Flat on the sheet was a brown scorpion body, crushed under the weight of them. In the mirror, she saw a red dot swelling at the base of her spine.

A year before she spent a semester abroad in Durango, Mexico. There were men there called alacraneros. She remembered seeing their trinkets. These men overturned rocks, dug the creatures out of the dirt and snatched them from people's homes to make souvenirs. Even nail salons there specialized in alacrán acrylics-ladies with inch long nails that have baby scorpions stuck under the gel.

When she walked up and down the stalls in a mercado, she stared at the bodies of these poor arachnids, crushed and commodified. There was an amber necklace with a light brown scorpion encased inside. She bought it for twenty pesos and fastened the silver chain around her neck because, then, it felt badass to have this once deadly thing hanging close to her heart. These were the months she looked back on, when she had always worn her wavy hair down no matter how hot it was, just to feel the strands being pulled from her sweaty neck to be kissed; those months when she never wore a bra and felt it was her right to keep nothing on but that necklace when she went to a new man's bed, insisting always on climbing on top so she could not be unseated. This was how she operated then, a mutual exchange in their territory, and then her, slipping away feeling powerful.

She liked the power of the necklace, though all her life she hated and feared scorpions. Their ugly bodies appeared all over her house as a child, and though she grew used to them living in the desert, she had always asked her mother to sweep them out of the house with the broom, too scared to do it herself. Living alone now, she was the one to sweep their furious little bodies across her doorstep like curbing the tide of sneaking invaders. When she returned from Mexico to begin her last semester of college, the scorpion necklace was tucked away in the dark of her drawer under her socks.

After that night, the pain in her spine increased and the dot grew larger. She didn't go to the doctor. It would be her fault for not protecting herself and her home better. It was just an irritated spot, she decided, and would heal soon enough with a cold compress. She was reacting to stress as the fall semester began to wind down. She didn't recognize her body's reaction. She couldn't sleep. When her body hair went smooth in patches and her skin started to harden into brown armor, she coated her body in aloe vera and took scalding showers. She only seemed to change faster.

She began skipping class. She covered the bald patches on her head with hats and wore baggy sweatpants to cover the bump on her spine.

Her nosy vecina in the apartment next door seemed to plan their encounters. Before that night, the old woman would hobble across the walk in her bata and house shoes to water the yellow patched lawn and offer to set her up with the old woman's handsome sobrino, "a good Christian boy." Now, the vecina let the water hose splatter her windows while she watched the girl pull her hoodie around her face when makeup no longer covered the darkening plates on her face. Once, she even dropped the hose onto the lawn and grabbed the girl's wrist with unbelievable strength.

—You don't look well. What's wrong?

—Not really your business ma'am.

Every instinct told her not to talk back to this woman, that although she was appraising her every time she went in and out the door, she was the only one to inquire if she was alright. Her question still came as an attack.

—Just that I haven't seen anyone come in and out since that young man left.

—Don't worry, you won't see much at all.

She broke the woman's grip and stumbled off, pulling her hood strings tighter. From then on, she always peered out of the window before leaving home to make sure her vecina wasn't hanging around. Had the vecina seen her changing pupils, the cracks in her skin? She couldn't take that chance.

A month after the attack on her body, she woke to find she could not peel her fingers apart; the skin of her hands was fused together. She could no longer steer a car. They were claws, bent and poised in defense.

Still, she did not go to the doctor. In the past, when she'd complained to the doctor in the campus health center about stomach aches and painful infections, he was quick to dismiss her pain and shove a prescription for antibiotics into her hand. The last time, when it hurt to pee, he had pressed her soft abdomen with his gloved hand so hard that she cried out. "It can't be that bad," he told her while she clutched the area where his fingers were. What would he say if she dragged herself into the clinic in this new form?

As a last resort, she walked to the house of a woman in her neighborhood that was known for conducting tarot readings and other healing rituals. She didn't know if she was a curandera or just another wispy, mysterious woman preying on her neighbors' superstitions. It was her only option, she thought She waited inside the woman's living room draped in red velvet hangings. A hundred flickering candles billowed and smoked around the room. The walls were covered in crosses and emblems from every religion she could think of, and she thought bitterly that at least her spiritual bases were covered.

When she was called to go to the back room--which was just the kitchen with a black woven tablecloth thrown over the kitchen table and candles around the perimeter--she sat across from the woman, who called herself Cleolinda, Linda for short, dressed in jeans and an oversized faded t-shirt. This was the woman who was supposed to read her fate?

--What can I do for you? Linda asked.

The girl removed her hoodie and shook her claws out from her sleeves to reveal her transformed self. Linda crossed herself, lit some incense on the table and wafted the billowing smoke around them both in what might have been a protective circle.

--My dear, what happened to you?

Here, she wanted to speak, but her words turned to scratches and clicks in her throat. She thought of the veiled judgement of older women that used girls like her as a cautionary tale. She sat back in silence. Linda leaned towards her to see past the scales on her face.

--Let's cast the tarot and see what the cards have to say.

Linda dealt the cards. Then, she flipped a select few over one at a time. The girl envied her nimble fingers despite the raised veins and age spots that covered them. She leaned forward to see the cards Linda turned over. The Empress, The Tower, 10 of Swords, Death.

--Don't be alarmed. The Death card does not mean physical death.

--What can it mean?

She was unsure whether Linda would understand her rasping and clicking.

--The Empress is your feminine power, your essential self. Death could suggest destruction, but with destruction always comes renewal, and sometimes even a fruitful decision. You are at a crossroads after a life-altering moment-the Tower. The sword can be destructive too, but it can also be your own defense. You may need to summon an inner strength and become more powerful. Does this mean something to you?

The girl nodded. She swept her pincer claws up and down her body to ask for a suggestion about what to do.

--Yes, I see. Your body is reacting to something, but I don't know what. Medicine may not help you unless you accept what is happening and why. There are no ointments or cures I can offer unless you admit to yourself why this is happening. Something festers inside you. Your body is defending against the pain.

The girl sat back in her chair and rested her claws on her lap. A strand of hair floated from her scalp onto her arm, the last of her hair.

—There's one more card here. The Moon. This can mean transformation, evolution, intuition.

—No more.

Linda did not charge her for her services. The girl could not have reached into her pocket either way.

Your black sting is raised above you when the men come into your home. You dig a hole through the cement where the floor of your room used to be.

They come in with weapons raised, probably because there is a smell, like damp rotting and all the curtains are down, but you keep burrowing past tile, cement and into the warm dirt beneath the place that was your house. Powerful claws, digging claws are what you have now, and they scoop and separate, dirt flying behind you, to create a space just right for your new body.

A voice follows behind the men; that woman who wanted to help and just couldn't seem to stay away. When they step on broken tiles behind you, they clatter. Your stinger is raised, but still you dig, even when one of the men picks up ripped clothes and locks of hair from the tumbled floor.

That was the girl you. The hard black plates of your back, your gigantic sting swaying overhead, is the only you left. They cannot hear your new name in your new voice, and you cannot remember the one they called you before. You crawl down into your hole and disappear into the earth.

SICK WOMAN TRAVELS TO DISTANT LANDS

You peel back the curtain. A swath of sunlight rides into the room and you remember what it was to step into the warmth of the sun without cringing, without fear of the flair across your eyes and then the pain.

You have been in bed for two days. There is the hunger that rumbles through your body, the need to feed yourself, but then the churning inside your stomach starts and makes your body want to get rid of everything and become a blank slate.

The world darkened when the virus spread. When you look outside, there are fewer kids playing in the street. People in masks rush by to get into their homes like they are reentering a clean zone, their homes the safest places to be.

You've been home. Home is a sanctuary when the body is not, but even then it can become an island, impossible to swim away from when your pain becomes a contagion people don't want to see.

On the night you come to me, it snows for the first time after a hundred years. A portal opens.

We meet on the snowy field at midnight, the winter moon full, casting light across the glistening whiteness. You walked here barefoot, peeling off your clothes until you arrived, naked and cool in the crisp air. You don't recognize me at first, but with time you will.

First you bow in front of me on your knees, arms bent forward and head down so that your frizzy hair sweeps the snow, leaving traces. When I bow my head to you, you know that you can climb aboard my brown hard shell and lay back across it like a starfish stuck to a rock. Your spine conforms to the curves of my shell. Your skin melts, becomes hot and sticky against me as we become one. All that we see are the tips of bare tree limbs and that full solstice moon watching us move slowly across the snow, back towards the portal to my world.

Your body has melded so seamlessly with my shell that you feel to me like a second spine, a layer of protection from the monsters of your world who would cage me or tear my shell from the rest of my body to consume me. This is why you don't scream as we cross the threshold, even as your naked skin turns from translucent white to red and begins to slough off of you into crisp layers that burst like a pollen bomb.

Your body is becoming something entirely different. I move slowly to take you away from yourself, back to my home where pain is a song, a story from another world.

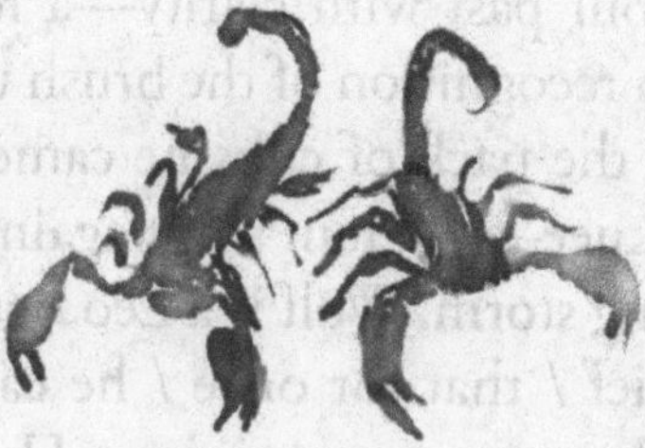

PART 2

CANCER MEETS LEO RISING

I stand in the rain and read Wolf his horoscope from the newspaper that is already a week late / he will not remember / there is something useful about seeing your past with clarity—a reverse fortune teller. He howls at my feet in recognition of the brush unturned / the places he never looked / for the pack of cubs he came from. Wolf pants / puts his head on my knee—the rain sings against our fur—wet skin waiting for the breaking storm. Wolf is a Leo / galloping here in bold anger and finding relief / that for once / he can roll onto his back and rest / he doesn't have to save someone. He doesn't know I was waiting to see my horoscope come true / that I was told to seek my lover in the woods on a rainy morning. The air after rain is insects buzzing home. I crumple the wet horoscope / let Wolf shake off his body and trudge off to a woodland floor waiting for his feet. Thirsty earthworms wriggle over my toes / aphids come to nest in my hair. I lay in the wet grass / imagine the whispers passing through roots beneath me.

Legacy

She was born with a supernova inside of her face. She cried inconsolably when it would shine and surge inside her cheeks but it wasn't until she turned 25 that her grandmother sat her down and explained that this starmass was smuggled in all the bodies of her foremothers when their galaxy was destroyed, and this was her legacy to bear.

Some days the starmass glowed consistently, burning through her face. But when it grew and glowed it set off explosions. On those days she couldn't go to work, couldn't even leave her bed, the pain scorched through her. Her grandmother always told her that this was a privilege to carry this piece of their past inside her body, but never told her about the unbearable bouts of pain. She never told her how to manage the pain besides with cold compresses of lavender oil and a dark room where the fiery glow of her face would light the darkness. She would burn so bright that she would float off the bed, levitating with the cosmos inside her.

Over time, the pain became too much to bear. She couldn't live her life this way. Friends who once gravitated around her were avoiding her calls. She used to go out dancing with them, but now she was confined to her home and there was never a day without pain.

Her doctors proposed an operation.

When the surgeon cut into her face and scooped out the light, it fell into their hand as a heavy, smooth piece of shungite, a black star mass like a hardened tumor. She carried the heaviness on a necklace around her neck and strangers reached for the smooth black stone and exclaimed how beautiful it was. Each time she touched its cold surface, she remembered the cost of relief.

SICK BED

A sickness in my brain is what they call my affliction.

Mother screamed at me when I could not move from the chair for days from the pain. I began pulling the thread of my sleeve until the sleeve was gone to my elbow and I had a pile of black thread in my lap.

Why would you do that? She asked.

I looked at the tangled mess of thread and handed it to her, tearing off the part still connected to my sleeve with my teeth.

It needed to come undone, I said.

This was why mother said I couldn't do anything of consequence, or make anything productive in a household if I was mad, or too sick to move. She said I was bent on destroying rather than making.

I asked her, was it can act of destruction to return a thing to its rightful form?

I only saw the bed as the needle was stuck into the crook of my arm and I fell back into the darkness again. They were throwing a sheet over the rubber that stretched the length of the tub. In my dreams, I floated on a pitch-black ocean.

It is difficult to pull the memory of my body on a boat from many years ago, but it surfaces and I remember how I heaved over the side of the boat all the eggs and toast and tea I had for breakfast that morning in a bitter mouthful into the foamy waves that broke against the wooden sides of the boat. This was the only time I was ever taken to sea, and that was enough. The bed doesn't feel that way, though I am confined to it. I feel carried by warm, gentle hands across waves that lift and push my body.

We are somewhere by the seaside. Seagulls cull out of the window and it smells damp and salty all of the time that I was awake and present in my mind.

I am allowed one hot bath a week when I can be alone.

I crave that time when I know no one else is going to scrub my skin raw or wait at the door and I can sink into the copper tub and shut my eyes.

There are hot springs, friends from school told me, where young people shed their clothes and swim naked in the hot water that smells of minerals, bodies coming together in the healing power of the springs.

In the bath, I think of us, slick bodies uniting together to hold one another, to kiss and caress each other, to laugh and play. It feels most natural to love my own body in the water, to cover my eyes with a wash cloth and dream that my fragile body is with them, being loved in the springs.

Every day the nurses roll my body from side to side to search for cuts, bruises and sores from lying still too long, or ones that were self-inflicted. I have learned not to thrash anymore, even when a gloved hand parts my legs and runs along my inner thighs.

The doctor's gloves taste of bitter medicine when he shoves a guard into my mouth (for the biting) and proceeds to pull my face apart looking for infections or malformations in my teeth until tears roll into my mouth and I choke.

When I close my eyes against the pain and grit my teeth, I wake to his wide smile and coffee-stained teeth bearing down on me.

"Very good," he says. "Very good."

All the while, my silence is his confirmation that I had finally become a model patient. Able to endure all and then some.

Mother says it may be time soon to come home. She wonders aloud, wrapping a knit blanket across my legs, if she will need to hire nurses to care for me there. A string sticks out the end where the blanket is fraying, and I hope for a day when I can pull my life apart in peace.

A Cautionary Tale

There is a rattling in the great hollow of my belly from the creature I swallowed   who keeps falling and falling inside me   screaming a name I don't know   the creature is running up my spine and flipping back over   filling my belly with burning   I know that they are choosing to scream and choosing to fall   this is the only story that they know   I swallow a match and hope that the swirling chasm of my belly does not extinguish the light   as I sit in the cave to eat my dinner and the creature inside me sits in the cave of me and reaches for the falling match   a torch in their world that wouldn't recognize the carvings on the walls of my belly from the other creatures that have fallen in and can't find their way out   of the story in my belly   they make up stories just to calm themselves at night around their campfires with their children   to tell them a tale of being stuck in the belly of a whale of a story that cares so little for them as long as they keep feeding me   if this is the story they want to tell and it will nourish my bones and keep me dry   then I let them yell and flip inside me   so long as they know that without my body forged word by word   they would be nothing   who came first, the light or the dark? Did the dark creep in before the light decided it needed to shine and   would there be a dark without a light or a light without a dark   this endless spinning made the universe explode and crash together to form a singular place where   creatures in my belly could feel safe   that they are trapped in the spinning smoke of a story

THE IN-BETWEEN MOTHER

Mother is teaching me to sing the sad songs of her people. She sings them from the cliffs overlooking the sea, and I want to know them but they are in her seal language. The language she never bothered to teach me, and father said that was best. I don't know the words but I know the tunes, so I hum along to her barking, rhythmic sounds. That's how we know she is a seal person, not just an animal. Her songs are neither here nor there. She sings more and more now that the seasons are changing, and I am old enough to learn.

When father returns from the sea, he likes to tell stories of storms off the coast and men overboard, but the story I want to hear most is how he took Mother for his bride. I sit at his feet near the heat of the stone fireplace and watch him light his pipe, the glow illuminating his weather worn fisherman's face. He rubs the stubble of his beard with the backs of his fingers, the friction churning the tale into being.

"I went to the bay where the fishermen say
The seal people dance in the dark.
There was your ma'
As naked as all
Frolicking round the fire and sparks
Her seal skin lay
On the rocks by the bay
So I took it up
And begged her to stay
By my side.
She obliged
And there we were wed
On the cliffs overlooking the bay."

He told all of his stories in verse, which I loved, but when he told this one, Mother would busy herself with washing dishes and lighting candles around our cottage; she seemed eager to escape the hearing of it.

"What did you do with Ma's skin?" I asked him each time, and each time he told me something different. This time, dishes clatter and Mother's head peers around the kitchen doorway to hear.

"It was mine to keep," is all he says. Mother's attention falls away, she returns to her duties, but I am sure she is on the lookout for her missing self.

Mother knits me a sweater as the weather turns cold, and we are housebound while Father is away at sea for days at a time. When he left, she pressed her cold cheek to his and kissed him. I wonder if she misses him when he is gone. We stay busy.

"These are the months my people would go away to warmer climes," she tells me from her rocking chair.

By her side, I brush the hair on my wood doll Samantha, who I named for myself. Her horse hair is slick and fine as my mother's silken locks, but Samantha does not get restless like Mother. She is content to sit in her wicker basket all day until I wish to play with her. Not so with Mother. When Father is away, she takes me to the cliffs and the beach more often. I imagine she is waiting to be rescued. I think of my far away grandparents, my seal parents, who must still be calling for her to return. The wind hums through her hair and she throws her head back, arms out and away. She could dive away, over the cliff at any moment. I croak for her. My bark and howl are unnatural. It scratches and dies in my throat, but Mother stops to comfort me, her unseal daughter. In the night, her candle flickers across the walls of my parent's room where I sleep in the warmth of their bed when Father is gone. She tells me stories of my grandparents and her sisters, who swim away in the winter and return in the summer to be near the shore, where the fish are. Her hand rolls through the air, mimicking the rolling body of the self she used to be. Her missing skin, she tells me, is the one thing that will make her whole.

"Have you looked for it?" I ask.

Her brown eyes spark in the light, but she doesn't say yes or no.

"You are old enough to know where your place is."

What does this mean? I wish I could find it for her, to see her beautiful seal-self restored.

Father is away longer this time and Mother is at the market, stocking up for supplies before winter winds come in full force. While she is away, I search the house for her skin.

The problem is I don't know what is should look like. I've only seen seals in the summer, lounging on the rocks in the bay. Will it feel like Father's rubber fishermen's boots or like my dolly's hair? Father's dresser and trunks hold only clothes and old photographs of his family who live three villages away.

Do they know he captured a seal woman for his bride? Do they know he had me? We've never talked about it.

The only place I haven't looked is underneath the floor. My hands shake when I take a hammer to the floorboards of their room and peel back the soggy wood. At first there is only dust and dead spiders but when I move their bed and pry away the floor, I find a suit of sleek brown fur that feels like skin. I hold it against my face and arms, try to slip my body into it, but it is much too big.

I wish to know my seal mother's embrace. Her love is a distant one, practical from day to day and weighed down with memories of her former life. Maybe I never knew her sadness until now.

Mother returns home with her basket full of new linens, wool for knitting, fat for cooking, flour and candles. I wait for her to remove her bonnet and shawl, to put up the groceries and come to her chair by the fire, the one she vacates for Father when he is home. Sitting in it is her skin, sitting upright like her second self. She stares at it for a time then takes it up in her hands, smells it, rubs it against her cheek and remembers. She starts to cry and drops to her knees. I come to her side and hug her shoulders.

I'm so proud to reunite her with her skin that seeing her cry over what she has missed doesn't frighten me. Mother hugs me back and continues to cry. I am crushed between her woman-self and her seal-self in a warm, slippery embrace.

Mother's scramble to the sea shore at dawn is how I learn she won't stay. Mother brings me too and lets me sit on the crystal sand of the beach while she strips off her clothes. The pale skin of her back disappears inside her dark brown seal skin as she rolls it over her shoulders, the head a hood that envelopes her face and makes her animal, though I know she isn't. The only part of her I recognize are her deep brown eyes now wide and set bulging from the seal head. Mother waddles towards the waves, looks back at me and dives away. When Father returns in two days, I am the only one left to tell him that she is gone.

In the spring, I tempt Mother back to me with fresh mackerel from a bucket, but she won't be fooled to separate herself from her skin again. Out of all her seal brethren, she alone heeds my whining call, the right cry this time. She nuzzles my hand and face, bends back and forth and barks for me.

Father asks how I know it is her. I know.

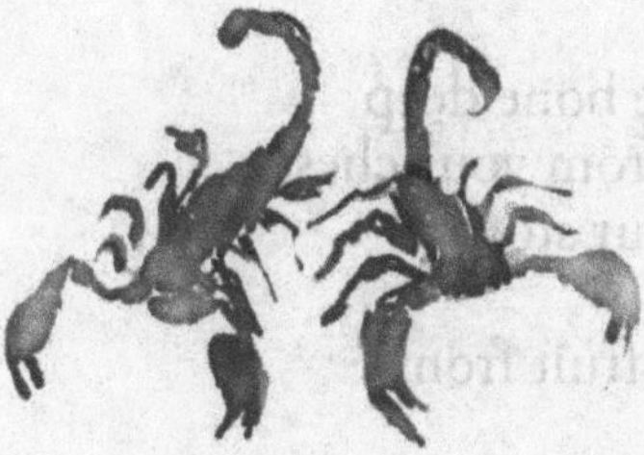

Part 3

LA ROSA

Don't make me your mother's cautionary tale, and I won't make you mine.

When we find each other, accept all that I have to give and take.

My thorns can plunge bone deep
and twist your heart from your chest,
but don't make that our story.

I don't have to be the fruit from
that illusive garden,
the siren calling from the rocks.

We can be us two together
no violence involved
as long as you accept my giving,
and my taking,
natural as the waves washing away and returning what you thought
was yours.

I can be your dream mujer
but never the waiting one,
the crying ghost dressed in white
that haunts rivers and crossroads for what she has lost.
I will not be tethered
I can settle like sediments on a rock
for a time
watch the city from the bus window
let you steer us to the way.

Always, I will return
to my original state of being
folded in on myself to prevent withering
drying out
bunched closed
waiting for the season
to open.

You will have to time the cycles
and hope you get it right,
pull your bleeding hand from my stem
and remember what your mother told you
about love's furtive flame.

THE SERPENT'S EYES

She smelled others who were lost, in bars, the dark courtyards empty at night except for those without a home, all places where people were abandoned. She walked in the darkness, ran her hands along stone walls, dry leaves, the heads of sleeping people on park benches. Their wounds called to her, though she had forgotten why.

Her wandering was endless. She had a fear that she wouldn't be able to find her way back. These nights she stalked for someone who would ignite her blood memory. Before dawn, she found him at a bar. His pallid face was slick with sweat and his pain dripped off of him like ceremonial oil. She sat next to him at the bar and ordered a drink, smiling in his direction.

"Want some company?" she scooted her chair closer. The man reared back, caught off guard.

"I'm a little tired, actually." His shoulders slumped forward.

"How about another drink?" The bottle in front of him was almost empty. She signaled for another, and when it came, the man took it.

"What's your name?" She asked.

"Elliot. And yours?"

"Some call me the Snake Woman."

Her eyes drew him in, black as the abyss of lost time. He straightened up to face her.

"What should I call you?"

"You can call me Male."

"That's different." He smiled now.

"Short for Maria Elena. Too demure for me."

She watched him tip back his drink, sensing the muscles in his back and shoulders loosening, relaxing into a comfortable heat.

"So," he said, "you like snakes?"

Male turned her back to him, sweeping the black curtain of her hair away to reveal her tattoos, the black serpents that draped down her shoulder blades. She rolled her shoulders where the skin stretched tight over meager bones. Imprinted on her shoulders were twin serpents, their black heads outstretched towards her arms and their black tails entwined where they linked at her back.

His hand reached out to brush a thumb across the snake's head. Her back rippled in response. Elliot peeled the sleeve of his t-shirt back like a broken scale to show his tattoo, a Celtic knot of thin green serpents, one consuming the other.

"They are beautiful. One life, one death, their fates locked together in eternity," Male said. She took another drink, suddenly thirsty.

"They are powerful," Elliot told her. "My snakes are my life."

"And how many snakes do you have?" she asked.

"Over fifty."

Male was thrilled at the prospect.

"I'd love to see them."

"Really? It's kind of late."

He was weary again, but when she put her hand on his shoulder, his starved body leaned closer, and he agreed to take her home with him.

His house was dark but Male could see every detail. She had driven his truck almost thirty minutes outside of town while he gave her blurry directions. He was giddy, taking too long to unlock the door and weaving his hand into the hair that swung at her back to steer her into the house. She tasted anticipation in his blood.

He guided her down the hall, past the small kitchen, the living room with a stained brown couch strewn with newspapers, and plates crusted with food and cups with stagnant water accumulating on the coffee table. The only area that was neat was one armchair, covered with a knitted quilt. In the kitchen, he popped open two bottles of cheap beer and they stood across from each other, her leaning against his sink as though she'd always been there.

"Sorry the house is messy," he said. He didn't really seem sorry. This, Male thought, was how he had been for some time.

"Can I see the snakes?"

The two reptile rooms were sectioned off from the rest of the house. The smell hit her before anything–the damp of wood shavings, soil, animal shit and decomposing. There was no blocking it out. She wouldn't want to.

He lit the first room with flickering florescent light. In this light, she could see just how doughy and raw his body was underneath the faded black t-shirt, as if he spent too long under this false light, too far from the sun.

As soon as the lights came on, snakes in their plastic enclosures began to bang against the glass, tales whipping, some even striking as they passed. Male noticed his affection for them, how he tapped the glass of each active snake and cooed 'hello there' and 'did you miss me?' at the unblinking eyes and open mouths. At first, she laughed at this display, but then she held her side and gasped in hurt.

He looked over as if he had forgotten she was there in his reverie of reuniting with them.

"I was out of town at a convention for snake breeders. I just got back tonight."

Elliot showed her each enclosure, the plastic containers and glass windows barely containing some of the bigger females. There was a cramped agitation in the room that made Male's skin itch.

"There's the green mambas, I have two in there. One female I was hoping to breed." He pointed to an enclosure. "In there is my treasure, a female West African Gaboon Viper. She's definitely the prettiest one I've got." The viper lay as motionless as a fat slug. Male got closer and the viper raised her pastel pink snout to peer back through the glass barrier.

"They're all beautiful," Male affirmed. The snakes who were awake watched them pass, and those who had been buried underneath their logs or dirt unfurled themselves, lifted their heads and stared.

"I think they sense someone new in the room," she said.

He nodded but stayed quiet.

"There hasn't been anyone else here but me for a while," he said. He looked to Male like someone lost, standing in the middle of the room that was his, and yet unseeing.

"They seem hungry," Male said.

"They can wait till tomorrow morning. It's their routine," he explained, making to switch off the lights.

"There's nothing routine about hunger," she told him and hugged her own stomach with memory.

She had not been inside her true form for some time. She was tired of wandering in this body. She wanted to feast, and remember.

He led her out of the snake room, back into the kitchen. He made her a bologna and cheese sandwich.

"I don't have much else. Not too good at shopping for myself these days."

She finished the sandwich in five bites so he made her another. This was not what she craved; white bread and synthetic cheese was a stand-in, a replacement for the kind of meal she had not had in a long time, but she thanked him anyway for his offering.

She glanced at the empty armchair, and the pink knit quilt.

"Who was here before?"

He followed her gaze. "My wife, Linda."

Male coiled up, staying very still, waiting for his explanation.

"We got divorced a year ago. It's been hard to get used to it. Sometimes I wish I'd given her as much attention as the snakes." Male pushed her chair next to his, not wanting to scare him off, and offered him her hand. His was warm, firm. A steady heart beat against her palm.

"Did she love your babies as much as you did?" she asked.

"At first. She loved the snakes too. Used to handle them, let them crawl all over her, while she folded laundry, while we watched TV, she even fed them by hand, the non-venomous ones. We didn't have kids for a long time, so they were our babies. But then it was so expensive to care for them, and I kept buying more dangerous ones. Then she got pregnant, after trying for a long time. She stopped helping me, avoided going into their rooms. Maybe she was scared." There were those tears again, openly leaking from this creature's eyes, and Male brought her face next to his, letting his tears rub against her skin. She wanted to swallow his entire being and shed him as a new skin.

"She lost the baby. Miscarriage. When she left, I realized that we never processed it together. I threw myself into caring for the snakes, and left her alone."

Male nodded, still holding his hand.

"I'm sorry to be like this. I've been alone for some time."

Male rose and walked to the armchair, sliding her hand across the quilt. Memory rippled into her consciousness, of Linda crocheting the quilt, of wearing it around their shoulders while they watched TV, a hand resting over her growing belly, of blood over the toilet, sweat and tears, and her hand smoothing the quilt over the chair when she left the house for the last time. The memory left Male back in the living room where he watched her.

"She left this behind. Why?" Male asked him.

"Don't know. Maybe it was her way to make sure I wouldn't forget our time together. She used to say that she balanced me out. Her softness with my boldness. We were kind of opposites that way. She was very different from you." His mouth was running again with beer and conversation. Elliot went to her and squeezed her hand. She savored his gratitude, even if it was not enough to satisfy her. Perhaps there was a way to teach him how to worship again.

But he had forgotten the care, the reverence in his hurry to cage and bottle up what scared him. He pressed himself to her back and reached for her hips so she could feel his need, but she was supple, moving away.

She asked to return to the snake rooms.

"Have you ever held them?" Male watched the two female Western Diamondbacks, their rattles shaking in agitation.

"I try not to. People get too comfortable with them, and that comfort is dangerous. I usually use the hooks when I want to take them out." He pointed to the different sizes of metal hooks and forceps hanging from the wall.

"Aren't they comfortable with you?" Male smiled.

"They're still animals."

"How do you breed them then?"

"It's a process. Tracking the female's cycle, temperature, finding a good male, and then I put them together in their own special enclosure and let them at it."

Male's lithe body slunk across the room, her black hair waving, to peer in at each snake in turn.

"Do they mate when forced?"

She pointed to one of the green mambas, who was watching her.

"Not yet. That one is stubborn."

The snake's small eyes watched her, filling her with the need to feel its body in her hands. It whispered to her and ran its brilliant nose against the plexiglass door.

"Can we feed them now?" Male pointed to the mambas.

"I don't think so. She's too fast to have two people in the room."

Though he swayed on his feet, she knew that he was sobering up, and needed to push the opportunity, to push past his fear. He feared his snakes, more than he knew, and had forgotten that fear and love walked hand in hand.

"I promise I'll follow your rules."

"If I do, you have to stand back, no sudden movements and never reach towards me or come close. Got it?" She nodded and placed herself at the other end of the room.

"I need to water them first."

He slid the cage door open and took a plastic squeeze bottle off the shelf. It had curved attachment that squirted water out of the tip, a crude nipple. Male watched as he sprayed droplets of water at the mamba's face. Her small mouth opened slightly while her throat gulped down water in a rhythmic motion. Her thirst was Male's thirst, her hunger, Male's hunger.

Elliot took the forceps from the wall and hooked a young dead mouse from the bucket, grasping its tail so that it hung upside down, its blood leaving droplets on the tiles. He dangled the mouse in front of the snake. Her head rose slowly, tracking the swaying of the mouse. He waited for small jaws to open, for the lightning strike that would launch her body forward.

The snake seemed distracted, placid when he wiggled the mouse's body in front of her. Its black pupil's watched Male approach and stand just behind him. Just as he turned to warn her back, the mamba shot out past the mouse and clamped down on his wrist. He felt the short fangs tag him once, twice, and then she disconnected. He fell to the floor and the mamba coiled back into her cage.

She placed a bare hand on the edge of the cage and let the mamba slither up her arm and cover her shoulders. The man's teeth clenched against the pain so hard she thought they might crack. Sweat and tears ran down his face, and she wanted to flick out her forked tongue and taste them.

There was no one to hold him, except the Snake Woman. He

peered up at her face, now skeletal and covered in white chalk, and the eagle feather armor that covered her body while she knelt beside him, the mamba still wrapped around her, and pulled him to her chest. Words tried to leave his mouth but were replaced with groans.

His dying body awakened her warrior self, her creator self who once ground bones into clay and blood to make human forms, and now wandered far from home. She remembered when she walked by the river at night, beckoning the dead women to follow her. She remembered the smoke that hung on the air for days, the smell of blood and tear streaked faces. She longed for her sister selves, to see her people sweep the house for the new harvest, to honor the midwife who ushered forth captive children from the womb. It came flooding back into her being, but she knew she needed more.

"Don't be afraid. This is the ritual." Cihuacoatl's sunken dark eyes roved over his anguish even as she held him.

"Whose?" He choked. She stroked the thin green body of the mamba draped around her broad shoulders.

"Our spirits are trapped at the crossroads, but you are bringing me back to my true form. You have tried to control the sacred, and now it is killing you. I can carry you across, if you are strong enough."

All of Elliot's words escaped as gasps.

"Who are you?"

"Everything."

The green head of the mamba bobbed on her shoulder, watching its captor's suffering.

Standing, she propped him up against the cages. His legs shook underneath him but he never stopped watching her. He could see the smoke swirling around them, smoke of battle, of the deathworld.

"Are you a demon? Am I being punished?"

She knew that he would have to wait for the venom to rush through him. Only between the worlds would he truly see.

"Help me release your snakes. They are hungry," Cihuacoatl said. The snakes' heads bobbed and stood at attention, warriors of the dead ready to bear witness to her becoming. The mamba still clinging to the curves of her shoulders, she watched him unlatch every cage in the room.

THE HUNGRY EARTH

"Kali in the Kitchen" by Tom Besson

The hungry earth opens, her howling voice pulls you in
You shouldn't be afraid, fall back into her arms
Your throat is a cave, full to the top with her care
where darkness falls into swirling sky
she cradles you, eternal mother, to her purging fire
peels your pain back from your bones
She flays you open, inside out babe
puts you back inside, born again from her many mouths
She knows when to push air past stubborn lips--
She washes you, wipes the blood from your eyes
breathes love into your name

CLEANSE

I remember the healer Grandma took us to in San Anto after our parents were killed. The woman rubbed us with an egg and smudged our bodies with smoke to cure us of our family's terrible luck.

There would be no ritual after your funeral. My last words to you were whispered against the wood of your coffin. I won't say them again. I hope you were listening then because I'm not coming back to visit your grave. That you in the ground stopped growing and expecting answers long before they buried you.

Our aunts needed time to debate about what they were going to do with me when they sold our house in San Antonio and moved Grandma to a retirement home. Auntie Minerva decided that I should live with Mommy's family for the summer. I hadn't seen them in five years.

I packed my small sketch book, that included that last drawing I did of you, and what few things I could bring in a duffle bag. Auntie Minerva dropped me off at the bus station to ride down through Laredo, Nuevo Leon, all the way down to Guerrero, where the family was waiting to pick me up from the bus depot in Ixtapa. I didn't fear leaving Grandma, changing buses in Monterrey, even being hassled on the bus because I look so Americana. I even slept without clutching my bag to my side.

When I stepped off the bus, I was hit with that humidity that makes even your insides sweat. Out on the street, Uncle Mando had the little blue truck parked out front and a sign that read "Bienvenidos Cristina." He pulled me into a moist embrace and I felt where his flimsy shirt stuck to his chest, like he'd been waiting awhile. "It's so good to see you," he whispered into my hair.

I stayed with Auntie Lucy for a month. I slept for days, rolling in out and out of dreams only to drink water. Then one morning she came into my room. I thought at first that she would sit softly on the side of my bed and rub my back through the blankets like Grandma used to when I was upset. Instead, she pulled the quilt out from under my tangled, sweating body until I stumbled onto the cool concrete floor. "Get up, Cristina." She waited while I stood in my tank top and underwear next to the bed while she folded the corners over and made it for me. When she left I pulled on my shorts before Humberto could burst into the room to tease me about my boy hips. Even after years of absence, I knew my cousin enough to remember his tricks. I went into the kitchen, the one room containing a sofa, a table and the gas stove in the corner, for breakfast. Auntie Lucy made huevos rancheros and fruit to tempt me to eat. She insisted I needed to gain weight. I ate half of my plate to please Auntie, knowing that as soon as Lucinda saw my clothes getting too tight, she'd tell me I was looking "gordita." I wanted to argue, like I would with Grandma, but the distance that had separated us for so long kept me from complaining that I wasn't hungry, that I wanted to be left alone to talk to you.

"What will you do today, Cristina?" Auntie asked me. She watched me like a balloon she was afraid would pop.

"Nothing," I croaked, my voice hoarse from too much sleep. Auntie frowned. "You're up now. You should try to make something of the day. You could help your Tio load the truck for the cows. You could play with Humberto. Take a walk."

The more activities she listed, the further I slumped down into my chair.

"Do I have to?" I couldn't remember the last time I had said something so whiney.

"Nobody is forcing you to do anything." She set a plate down hard in front of me and salsa slopped over the side onto her white embroidered tablecloth.

I didn't come back to her easily.

When I grew tired of company, I climbed trees by the arroyo that bordered the property to draw plants I didn't remember and the lazy sleeping figures of the iguanas perched on the branches that hung towards the water. I missed Sunday night football, all of us on the couch rooting for the Cowboys. I missed keeping up with the weekly comics I used to draw for my friend Ashley. I missed having a way to reach out to people, but if I'm being honest, I stopped doing that even when you were alive.

Though he annoyed me, I appreciated Humberto, who liked to steal my sketch book and hide my things. He treated me as he always had. At least his mischief was fair.

One night Auntie and I were alone. She brought out a round hat box full of pictures for me to look through at the kitchen table while she made caldo de res. It was one of those long summer evenings when the sun takes its time descending behind the mountain. Some of the pictures were of Grandma and Grandpa from years ago, of their daughters, including Mommy. There was one of you, sent from Victoria, the inscriptions on the back reading "Angelina, tres años." There was one of Mommy and Dad's wedding there. She was wearing a lace dress with a sweeping train. I held the photo of them over the steam of the pot. "Look how beautiful Mommy looks in her dress," I said.

Auntie moved my hand away and took the picture. "We were all so happy that day," she said. Her face hung over the pot, the steam drawing out each line, and her eyes tilted up like the paintings of holy saints looking towards the heavens with mingled anguish and hope.

"We missed you, Auntie," I told her.

She put her arm around my shoulders, both of us sweating near the boiling pot. "I missed you too, Cristina. You and everyone. Too many of us are separated. Some here, others allá en el otro lado." She meant her sisters across the border. But I thought of the borders between space and time, where you and our parents might even now be reunited.

"When you have a family, you'll know what it is to give up certain things for them," she added, stirring the broth in the pot while I poured the onions and cilantro in, and we remained standing side by side until the stew was ready to serve. This was one of those moments I knew I wouldn't soon forget. Memories can be as persistent as ghosts. I remember the day you came into the room, clutching yourself the way little boys do. You said it burned. "Come see," you told me, taking my hand. In the toilet, there was bright red blood floating in little rosettes like watercolors on wet paper. After weeks of tests, the rounds to the clinic, then urologists, Grandma ushered us to a specialist's office to explain your condition. End stage renal failure.

The first thing you asked the doctor as you peered up into his bearded face was "will there be needles?" Grandma hid her face in an embroidered handkerchief Auntie Minerva sewed for her. Outside the office we waited for Grandma to pull the car around. It was the kind of day you loved, bright sunshine and grass so green it reflected light. You said "look!" and showed me a monarch butterfly perched on a dandelion that swayed in the wind. Its filmy wings fluttered and there was no urgency in either one of you. You watched that butterfly until it tilted backward in the wind and took off, and you ran to follow it, trying to clap your hands around it to keep it from flying away. Nothing in your flushed face, your rhythmic leap and descent said your blood was poison, recycling impurities through your cells, killing you slowly.

After I'd been back with the family for a while, Uncle Mando's brothers and all their kids and wives came into town to celebrate my return to Mexico. Our tias spent hours cooking carnitas, making fresh tortillas, smacking balls of rolled masa between their hands to make gorditas. Most of these women I hadn't seen for years, some of the kids I'd never even met. I humored them with hugs, but they wanted to press me to their sweating bodies like I could be reabsorbed. The already crowded house overflowed onto the front porch. I went to sit underneath the avocado tree to watch the commotion from afar. Our cousins chased the chickens across the dusty yard and antagonized the ancient donkey, Berto with sharpened sticks. I watched everything happening like I was looking through a small window at their lives. Our prima Lucinda came with a beer and sat next to me beneath the tree. She came home from school just for this party. Her brother waved to her as he poked Berto again near the tail, narrowly escaping a kick from his powerful old hoof.

"Avoiding everyone again?" She waved her bottle to warn Humberto away from the donkey.

"I'm glad everyone could come," I said.

"Anything for a party," She took a big swig from the bottle. "You're not talking much like you used to."

"You haven't seen me in a long time. Maybe this is me now."

"Maybe. But I doubt it."

The light from the canopy hit her face and I said "hold still." I took out my sketch book, and started to draw the lines of her shoulders, her sweeping black hair dyed that ridiculous blond and her full lips. Despite years of tweezing there was still a sweep of fine black hair above them. Noticing that I was drawing her, she sat very still and gave me an expression of absolute seriousness, not her usual puckered kiss that she would give to a camera. We sat there as I drew her, ignoring the sounds of the birds overhead or the buzzing of mosquitos and dragonflies. When I was done, I ripped the drawing out of my notebook, dated it and handed it to her.

"Keep it," Lucinda said as she pushed the picture back to me. "When I'm famous you can sell it."

I folded the picture back into my sketchbook, laid my head on Lucinda's shoulder and she swept the hair from my forehead.

"You'll be alright chamaca. Even if you aren't right now." She reminded me of when we were still little, the first few times we came to visit Auntie Lucy's family. We still fell into the same rhythm, no matter how much time had passed. I understood that they could not gather the money to come to your funeral.

"I'll be better when I'm not here."

"That's a shitty thing to say," Lucinda said. She was smiling.

"I mean, I love your mom but…"

"I get it. You should come live with me. I have a pretty big apartment now since my roommate moved out."

I took the bottle warming in her hand and took a bitter sip.

"If you say so."

Throughout the afternoon we snuck swigs of tequila from the gigantic curved bottle that Uncle Mando's brother brought from Aguascalientes. It helped that I stuffed down three gorditas full of that sweet, marinated meat that spent hours simmering on the stove. Someone was playing cumbias on their phone, and we kicked up dirt trying to keep up with the steps.

We came together at the two long tables pushed together to accommodate everyone. Uncle Mando raised a glass to me. They thought that to toast my health was be a talisman of sorts, to protect me from the bad luck that has ravaged our family. Whether I believed it or not, I raised my glass, shouted out "salud" and drank down the wine in my cup.

Walking down the street through the barrio towards town with Lucinda makes me feel like I am walking in the shadow of a parade. All the vecinos say hello and all the men take a second glance. In my khaki shorts and sandals, no one is looking at this güerita, as they love to call me. If it isn't for her pushing me to accompany her on daily errands, I might not have left the house at all. But she got me drawing again.

Drawing Lucinda was the first time I considered drawing someone other than you. I liked drawing you when you had to sit for hours, hooked up to that huge, whirring machine, tubes coming out of you and into you to receive your dialysis. You laughed when I passed the time by drawing you. Sometimes like a cartoon, with your eyes bugging out. Once I drew you as a superhero cyborg, in which the dialysis machine transformed into your protective suit. The time I remember most was when you said, very seriously, "Draw me like I am right now." I finished that drawing over a series of visits to the clinic, trying to remember where I left off so that I could change little details here and there to make it seem like it was just one moment, when it really stretched out a year and a half. Your sickness was a part of our life by then. Grandma pulled you out of school. "I can do better with her at home," she explained to the principal. I used to think that if I had been in your place, I would have slacked off to watch cartoons. When you threw a fit and tossed your pencil down because you hated long division, Grandma was the one to set down her spoon as she cooked dinner and prop you up again. I can confess to you now that I didn't want to come home to you. I stayed out playing basketball with my neighborhood friends, even if they weren't really my friends because they didn't ask after you. I would walk to the corner store for snacks I couldn't afford just to avoid home for a while. Grandma tried to notice, but you were her full-time job.

In my last drawing of you your face is swollen. Your black hair falls down to your back, you have those furry little eyebrows you were too young to care about and beneath them, those clear brown eyes, daring me to look away.

Sometimes in the morning, Lucinda poses for me while she drinks her coffee and flips through her textbooks. At night, we sit out on the patio. I admire the smoke of Lucinda's cigarette and the dark overhang of the tree that protects the people passing underneath us. There's something about floating above people like ghosts that made me feel closer to you, and yet there was Lucinda next to me, watching right along with me.

To help Lucinda pay rent, I got a job at the local supermarket. They let me stock shelves, price items, and sometimes work as a cashier, though people's accents throw me off, and I have trouble remembering the right words. I got so flustered my first week, trying to make change while a mother with her three kids waited with an outstretched hand that I dropped all her coins on the floor. Then my manager Javier put me on stocking duty. Andres, one of my coworkers, comes and visits me sometimes when I am stocking. He likes how clueless I am and likes to help me.

"You know, usually people don't migrate to Mexico from the US. Most times it's the other way around," he says, handing me a box of cookies to put on the shelf I'm busy stacking.

"It wasn't exactly a choice."

"Yeah, it isn't for others going to el Norte either."

I feel my face growing red.

"Phew, she gets riled so easily," he teases. "Have you gone out since you've been back? We go dancing after work on Fridays if you want to come."

"Have you seen my coordination?" I say, making to catch the precarious boxes as if they might fall. He grabs my hand and tries to dip me, laughing. This is a boy who would only be too happy to grind on me at a party and let me drink too much. How was I supposed to know that once you were gone that I would have to build a life outside of you?

A little girl with long black hair and red shoes runs shrieking down the aisle, and I fall to my knees, Andres falling down with me. That little girl barely looks like you, but her laugh runs through my body because I haven't heard your high-pitched shriek in so long that my ears don't remember you.

"You ok?"

I let my palms rest against the freezing, stained tile and breathe hard through my mouth. Then I nod.

"Yeah. Let's finish up here."

After that, I'm cool with Andres, but I avoid being alone with him if I can. He pushes too hard. I wait for him to put up the rest of the boxes and leave to work the cashier before I rest my forehead against the shelf and hope that no customers come down the aisle to see me falling apart.

I don't tell Lucinda about Andres or how my co-workers are even more skittish around me than before. But on a weekend when neither of us are working, Lucinda decides that we both need to get out of town. We are going to catch the three-hour charter bus to Acapulco for the day. "We're gonna have so much fun!" she reminds me, as if I need convincing. Lucinda falls asleep an hour in, leaving me to stare out the window at the palm trees flashing by, road side stands filled with papayas as big as my arm, the Toyotas two decades too old driving alongside us.

When we get to Acapulco, she is quick to study her reflection in the window and wipe the small line of drool from her cheek. "¡Que horror!" she exclaims at herself. We walk through the bus terminal to the entrance outside that opens onto a side street. Acapulco is all tourists and wide city streets where the only trees growing are the palm trees hanging over street vendor's stands. It is just as hot there as where we left, so we stop to get snow cones to cool our dry throats. As we walk, she points out all of the nightclubs popping up, the new resort hotels that no one is staying in now because even in Acapulco, Americans think it isn't safe to visit. I laugh at the lines streaming into the Wal-Mart's, the Costco's, so much of home there that I feel like crying. "Oh yeah, they love that stuff," Lucinda says, dismissing the monstrous box stores which give the skyline an appearance of modernity that falters next to old women selling fruit in plastic bags.

Lucinda takes me to a city park with a laguna full of dirty water where we rent a paddle boat, chasing gooey-eyed couples and splashing them. I'd forgotten how much I liked my cousin; for all her swagger, she is fun. As we float across the surface of the pool, watching the dragonflies circle around us, she lights a cigarette and offers me one. I shake my head no. It's been hard to get used to her smoking. Grandma quit years ago and slapped one out of my hand when I was little and pressed it between my lips to taste the smoky sweet tobacco inside.

Lucinda lets the smoke swirl out of her pink painted mouth, showing her yellowing teeth and taps the cigarette against the side of the plastic boat. The ashes slide away on the surface of the water.

"I needed this," she sighs. "Midterms are killing me." She is taking summer classes to get past her prerequisites.

"Oh yeah. Sitting in the lap of luxury." I lean back far enough for my hair to dip into the dirty water and she slaps my arm.

"No seas pendeja." I roll my eyes.

"You seem better to me."

"Maybe." I don't like to let Lucinda take credit for moments of my happiness.

"Do you think you're going to stay?"

I wasn't expecting this question and the boat wobbles when I straighten up.

"I ask because I want to know I can count on you sticking around for a little while. You're helping me out and…I think I am helping you too."

"How am I helping? I make enough to buy food. That's about it."

Lucinda smiles.

"There's other ways to help. The dishes were never this clean before." Now I slap her arm until she laughs. "It's been hard to live alone, away from the family. It's been nice to have you around. You could do more here. Come take classes with me."

I didn't finish my junior year of high school. I wouldn't even know where to begin.

"I think I should be able to decide what happens to me. That feels important now," I tell her. Lucinda stubs out the cigarette and throws it in the water.

I think of you and how many times I had failed to be present when you needed me, and whether you would be jealous of my time with Lucinda.

I hop out of the boat at the bank, and then allow Lucinda to grab my hand before she tripped on her heels. We stroll through the rest of the park where a makeshift zoo is set up. There are rusting cages full of toucans and other brilliant birds, a rock and a little pool for three long alligators, and last, one cage, no longer than twelve feet, for a black panther. Several kids crowd around the cage while the panther sleeps. Their parents are busy buying ice cream cones. They chatter around the cage, holding onto the bars and tossing in pebbles. He is sleek as night, the only thing to give him away are those glowing yellow eyes. Lucinda goes to buy a Coke, and I stand behind the taunting kids to watch the sleeping animal. His eyes are crusted, his black coat dusty from the red dirt kicked up around him. When one pebble hits the rock where he is sitting, he opens one bright yellow eye. Whether he pleads for peace, or for the child to come a bit closer, I am not sure because he closes the magnificent eye a minute later. I sit on the bench by the cage, waiting for Lucinda, staring at the panther. I think of you again, before they closed your casket and your funeral started. Your hair was polished obsidian, cascading around your arms along the silk casket lining. Unlike our parents, you did not need as much makeup, so you looked almost like yourself. In the endless minutes before the service began, I stood beside your casket with Grandma to receive the handshakes of each nameless visitor. If I stared hard enough, I could imagine your chest rising and falling beneath your green satin dress.

The panther's fur and your hair blend for a moment. Lucinda puts her arms around me and leads me away from the cage. I can't see my face, but it must have begun to crumple into that ugly expression I make when I'm coming undone. "I'm sorry," she keeps muttering in my ear. I wonder what for.

The ability to beg is beyond me now. There is nothing that I want enough to beg for it. I begged for you. For months after your diagnosis I would come home after school and go straight to my room, unable to say hello to you. I imagined you standing on the other side of the door, though I never checked. I left the light off, lay my backpack on my chair next to my desk and sat on the bed, feet planted on the floor. My hands would run up and down the comforter and make a static rhythm that seemed trancelike. In world history class we read about meditation, how if you center your thoughts on one idea, that you had the potential to heal yourself. If I did the same, centered my mind on healing you, you would live. I closed my eyes, pictured your face and moved my hands back and forth across the bed. My whisper was barely a breath I repeated over and over, falling into a state only Grandma could bring me out of when she called me to dinner. I can't tell you what I whispered, what my mantra became. Some things are private.

Grandma never took us to church, not since we went to live with her. She prayed the rosary at home locked in her bedroom. As many times as you tried to listen in on her prayers and I kept you away. Grandma had her own questions she wanted answers to. I think of her in the nursing home and wonder if she would recognize me now, though I still look the same. Auntie Minerva tells me that when she visits, Grandma still asks for you, forgetting that you're gone. I do miss sitting on the edge of her bed while she reclined, her eyes barely focused on the TV across the room as she napped, to hold her wrinkled hands, running my thumb across the raised river of veins that are comforting to know still flow with blood untainted. I don't know if Auntie tells me this to make me feel guilty. They prefer I would scream and shout than not know what I'm thinking. She tries to put Grandma on the phone, and I say no. It is easier to be away than to hear Grandma whisper your name in my ear.

Lucinda took me to Sunday Mass once. The skin under my hair was damp with sweat as I knelt in the pew. The priest compared the Lord's love to an undying flame, one that can always be rekindled inside us if only we ask for his intervention. I felt the flames, the heat in my cheeks, and ran my hands up and down the legs of my jeans, trying to find the soothing rhythm I used to have. I refused to take communion. The priest offered me the proffered cup but I kept my lips sealed. Your blood Angelina, unclean, filtered through a machine, poisoning your undeveloped body. I refused to drink the blood of sacrifice. You were no sacrificial lamb.

I visit a curandera instead, like Grandma would have done.

This woman is kind. Her grey hair is in a beautiful braid, and she reaches for my face first, holding it for a long time. I don't pull away. Though I don't understand all of her instructions, she shows me how to build an altar with pictures of you, and your beaded necklace, the last thing I have of yours. The curandera tells me to put you in the West, where the dead live, to surround you with the four elements. A cup of water, copal to burn, candles, a deep purple amethyst Lucinda bought for me in Jalisco that is supposed to bring calm. She tells me to pray your name into the candle's flame, that with each word to you, I will call you into being.. Even though she doesn't agree with me on this, Lucinda let me use an entire table to set it up in my room and put the stone there herself.

I am instructed to perform a ceremony, and Lucinda encourages me. I am supposed to burn sage in the space, to say your name like a prayer, and meditate, envisioning your face, and leave your soul in the past where it is supposed to rest. "You've brought a lot of bad memories with you. This will help you let go," Lucinda explains.

Lucinda means well, but she has never lost like me. The pictures of her parents, of Humberto and her friends from college are reminders of a life lived in happiness, and hopefulness. She has been so patient, yet I am still a problem she wants to find the solution to. She tells me I can enroll in school like her, to do what I don't know. I can't begrudge Lucinda her request when her entire energy is bent towards creating her best chance.

When I am tucked under the sheets at night, I still feel your warm body next to mine, the way we used to sleep together when you were scared of the shadows coming in through the window. You rolled over, hugged my back and whispered "I'm not afraid Cristina," casting that statement into the universe to protect us both.

I prepare to light the sage, to let the smoke lick the corners of the ceiling, to close my eyes and concentrate on leaving you where you belong. In the end, I stick the bundle back in a drawer. I tuck you away inside me like silk folding over a ruby, careful not to scuff or break my memories of you.

THE WAYWARD SISTERS

<u>Sisters in Exile</u>

We were born for sorrow.
On the hill where three roads meet,
find me there when we are lost to one another.

Witch they have called me.
Bad woman
taken from one another for seeing truths
and telling them.

I cross the moors
hugging my shawl around my shoulders.
When will we three meet again?

<u>Seeing Signs</u>

In the meeting place
wild dogs harken to our coming
They will say we have come.

We will stretch our spindly fingers
and stand together
strong against our attackers,

conjuring fortunes in our hearts.

Strange men who wish to know their destinies
wait under cover of darkness
to fulfill their own prophecies
of violence to the world.

The Sisters Return

Doorways open at the crossroads,
here the spirits speak our stories
the ones even we cannot know.

We take hands and recite in the dark
our spell of affirmation
that we are the progeny of worlds gone by.
We have come and gone
when earth cracked and oceans boiled
and no violence of man
will keep us from each other.

Resources towards Writing the "Weird"

In the process of writing this book over the course of several years, I was inspired time and again by other stories, novels, TV shows and creators who were constantly pushing me to consider what storytelling could be and what incorporating and blending genres of poetry and prose, horror, folktales and traditional stories, as well as magical and speculative imaginings could mean for my work.

Here is the list of works that influenced *Las Criaturas* and/or that inspire me:

1. *Women Who Run with Wolves: Myths and Stories from the Wild Woman Archetype* by Clarissa Pinkola Estés

2. *Itza* by Rios de la Luz

3. *Her Body and Other Parties* by Carmen Maria Machado

4. *SanTana's Fairy Tales* by Sarah Rafael Garcia

5. *Freshwater* by Akwaeke Emezi

6. *Cuicacalli: House of Song* by ire'ne lara silva

7. *Wound from the Mouth of a Wound* by torrin a. greathouse

8. *The Carrying* by Ada Limón

9. *Three Scenarios in Which Sasaki Grows a Tail* by Kelly Luce

10. *Pretty Monsters* by Kelly Link

11. *Eat The Mouth That Feeds You* by Carribean Fragoza

12. *Penny Dreadful* (TV Series)

13. *Supernatural* (TV Series)

If you are looking for ways to dig into the weird in your own writing, here are few prompts to get you started or help you on your way:

1. Think of a traditional story or folktale that you have heard many times before. This story could be from the lore of your family, your culture or an urban legend or cautionary tale. Write the story out in direct address, telling the story to an imaginary reader (practice telling it aloud first). What would a conversation with this story look like/sound like/be like? Would there be push back from the story about the way you tell it, or from the person who has told it to you many times? How might the story change to suit your needs?

2. Write a story about finding an object, like a shirt, a drinking glass, or a journal at a thrift store. If this object were imbued with a power, what would it be? What is the story behind this power? Create a character who could wield it, or imagine one who tried to wield this power and fails.

3. Imagine your body begins to transform against your will. How would this transformation change you? What was living inside of you that made this transformation necessary?

Acknowledgements

Thank you to all of the wonderful people who believed in and encouraged my weird little stories and poems that have developed into this book over the course of the last four years.

Thank you to Edward Viduarre and FlowerSong Press for taking a chance on my book in the first place and welcoming me into the FlowerSong Press comunidad. All gratitude to the amazingly talented Elaine Almeida for her work creating the beautiful cover for this book.

Much thanks to the editors and journals that published poems and stories from this collection: Laura Pegram and *Kweli Journal* for publishing "Cleanse", *BorderSenses* for publishing "The Monster," Megan Giddings and the editorial team at *The Offing* for publishing "La Mujer Alacran," *Lumina* for featuring "Offering to the Sky," *NILVX: A Book of Magic* "Ancestors" anthology for publishing "The Wayward Sisters," and the *I Scream Social Anthology Vol. 1* for publishing "La Rosa." In addition, thank you to the University of Houston PhD in Spanish program, my friend Ana Leticia De Leon and Lucero Hernandez for turning my story, "The Monster," into a chapbook, and to LibroMobile for re-designing and printing that chapbook as part of the LibroMobile Press zine series.

I am grateful to the *Winter Tangerine* "Feathered We Remember" workshop for inspiring some of the work in this collection and the enduring community of the "Writing Life Retreat" I had the opportunity to be a part of, created by ire'ne lara silva.

Thanks to my professors and thesis committee at Texas State University's MFA program for all your work and feedback on this collection from its inception, especially Jennifer duBois, Dr. Nancy Wilson, Dr. Robin Cohen and Dr. Geneva Gano.

I want to give my enduring love and thanks to my mentors, friends and community members who have shown me ways forward and challenged me to imagine what is possible in my own writing, Sarah Rafael Garcia, Marilyse Figueroa, Natalia Sylvester, ire'ne lara silva, Rios de la Luz, Claudia Cardona, jo reyes boitel, Heather Lefebvre, Carolina Hinojosa-Cisneros, Kermit O, Micah Ruelle, and Katrina Goudey.

To my mother Christi, who read my early work and always encouraged me to keep writing. To my stepfather Daniel, my sisters Maddison and Alissa, my wonderful cousins and my grandparents who came to my events and were excited for me as "the writer of the family."

And always, to my husband Ramiro, who has supported my work, my random writing bursts, my many readings and events and my addiction to Supernatural and Penny Dreadful with love, humor and patience. Te amo por siempre.

Biography

Leticia Urieta is Tejana writer from Austin, TX. She works as a teaching artist in the Austin community. She is a graduate of Agnes Scott College and holds an MFA in Fiction writing from Texas State University.

Her work appears or is forthcoming in *Cleaver*, *Chicon Street Poets*, *Lumina*, *The Offing*, *Kweli Journal*, *Medium*, *Electric Lit* and others. Her chapbook, *The Monster* is out now from LibroMobile Press.

She is fueled by sushi, pug videos and ghost stories.

https://leticiaaurieta.com/

@LeticiaUrieta

9 781953 447838